MW01229080

PREACHING ESSENTIALS

BY CHAD MEZA

FOREWORD BY BOBBY AMEZCUA

Preaching Essentials

ISBN: 978-1-300-63828-5

DEDICATION

To my son, Micah Cayden Meza, may you preach the Gospel with excellence, glorifying the Lord Jesus Christ across the whole world.

CONTENTS

FOREWORD

What does "preaching" look like? To some, it may be how sweaty one can get while doing it. To others, it may be getting very loud and looking mad, while others may seem timid and overly humble. There are so many variations of "preaching", I cannot cover them all here. Everyone likes what they like, and will attend a church where they like that pastor's style of preaching.

Preaching, however, is not just a question of style, but of substance and effectiveness in putting forth God's holy Word. Is your preaching being as effective as you desire it to be? Is your preaching correct and in context of the scriptures?

We understand that His Word does not return void, and the Holy Spirit is able to get "the message" into the listeners' hearts supernaturally. But, I also believe that the hearer of our preaching should hear the Word with clarity and correctness. Jesus did not use His words out of context, nor did He say things just to make Himself look good and become popular. Jesus was not concerned that His preaching may offend someone. He preached truth, and He preached it effectively. He was about His Father's business, and His Father's agenda, not His own.

Unfortunately, I believe too many preachers today try to make the non-believers so comfortable and welcomed, that the truth is preached so blurred that one can barely tell if we are hearing the true preaching of the Gospel, or simply involved in Christian entertainment.

I believe that Christ, our King, has redeemed us to accomplish His will. He has called us to be the preachers of His holy Word. Since our King calls us to do so, shouldn't we do it with excellence? Shouldn't we invest in ourselves to become continuously better than we are now? Our church size and our comfort should not be the determining factor as to where we stop trying to better ourselves as public communicators, which is exactly what we are. The better communicators we become, I believe the more doors the Holy Spirit can open for us – effectual doors, where the hearers behind those doors only listen to certain kinds of speakers.

With that said, I highly recommend this book to everyone who desires to attain excellence in their service to the Lord in any capacity requiring public communication – especially Pastors, Evangelists, Apostles, Prophets and Teachers. *Preaching Essentials* contains simple, but valuable nuts and bolts to communicating the Gospel in a more excellent way. It challenges one to grow in the area of study, preparation, and delivering a good message to edify the Body of Christ and present to non-believers the Gospel of salvation, effectively. No one can go awry using this valuable tool to enhance one's own preaching of the Gospel. Yes, I do understand the bottom line is that this "work" is in fact the work of the Lord and He can use anybody, anywhere. But what does that have to do with you improving who you are in Christ? Strive to serve God in a more excellent way my brethren. Invest in yourself to become a better preacher.

- Pastor Bobby Amezcua
Activate Church, CA

INTRODUCTION

What makes a sermon good? What makes a preacher effective? Is it the kind of clothes they wear? Is it the way they project their voice? What is it?

Truthfully, I think we can have all the charisma in the world, and still deliver an ineffective sermon. By the same token, I believe we can have the "deepest" content, and yet, still deliver an ineffective sermon.

The best sermons, the most effective sermons, are those which connect with the listeners. They are clear, organized, engaging, and most importantly, they are rooted in the truth of God's Word. This requires good sermon preparation and good delivery. And that's exactly what we're going to focus on in this book.

In the first section of this book, we'll cover everything you need to know about preparing for a sermon, from selecting a main passage of scripture to actually writing out a sermon. You'll learn proven methods and best practices that will help you organize, outline, and write an effective sermon.

In the second section of this book, we'll devote our time to sermon delivery. It is in this section that you'll learn incredibly practical tips to help you deliver your sermon effectively. Whether you are already comfortable speaking in front of others, or whether the thought of being in front of people scares you to death, this section will serve as an invaluable resource for improving your public speaking skills.

I commend you for taking this next step to better yourself as a preacher. Pursue excellence. Be the best preacher that you can be. To God be the glory.

SECTION 1:
SERMON PREPARATION

1. SELECT A TEXT

The first stage of sermon preparation is selecting a text, or a passage of scripture, to preach from. Every sermon should be anchored in one main passage of scripture. That doesn't mean you cannot include other verses; it just means that there is a central passage that is the main drive and focus of the sermon.

Why is this important? Because effective sermons are rooted in the truth of God's Word. We want to preach God's Word, not ours. We don't want our sermons to be based on our ideas, where we take our ideas, and use a bunch of scriptures to just say what we want to say. Rather, we want our sermons to be based on what the Bible says. We want to choose a passage of scripture, and then teach what that passage says.

So, how do we select a main text for our sermon? There are a few ways you can do this:

1. Select a passage you had in mind already.

2. Start with a topic, or an idea, and find a scripture that deals with that topic.

3. Continue where you left off last.

Let's review each of these options briefly.

WHEN YOU ALREADY HAVE A PASSAGE IN MIND

There are times you already have a passage of scripture in mind to preach from. Maybe you were assigned a passage to preach from, or maybe you just had something on your heart. In this case, you're all set.

WHEN YOU ARE STARTING WITH A TOPIC OR IDEA

Sometimes, you may not necessarily have a particular scripture in mind, but you might have a topic or an idea that you want to work from. You still want to choose a main text. One thing you could do is use a concordance to look up passages that include certain words. Often, you can find a concordance in the back of your Bible. Otherwise, you can use a standalone Bible concordance (e.g. The New Strong's Expanded Exhaustive Concordance of the Bible). You can also use free online resources like the keyword search on BibleGateway.com. So, if you wanted to talk about "faith", you could do a search online or use a concordance to find scriptures that talk about faith. Doing this search, you might decide to use something like Hebrews 11:1 as your main text.

WHEN YOU ARE CONTINUING WHERE YOU LEFT OFF

Some people prefer preaching verse-by-verse through sections or books the Bible. If this is what you're doing, you simply want to pick up where you left off last. Basically, if you just preached Galatians 5:19-21, then you would pick up on the next verse and preach Galatians 5:22-26.

HOW LONG SHOULD THE MAIN PASSAGE BE?

When selecting our main scripture, one question to consider is how many verses should we include? When selecting a passage from the Bible, you generally want to use as many verses as necessary to develop an immediate context. If you are reading from a Bible version like the English Standard Version (ESV), you may find that preaching a paragraph of verses at a time, or more, works quite well.

For instance, you probably would not want to preach Job 1:4 as a standalone scripture. But rather, you would want to use Job 1:1-5 as a single unit, to develop context. And even then, Job 1:1-5 is simply a background for the story that follows. Therefore, a preacher might choose to minister from Job 1:1-12 or even Job 1:1-22.

On the other hand, there are certainly times when a preacher will only use a single verse as the main scripture for a sermon. When dealing with a narrative in the Bible (e.g., the story of Joseph in Genesis), you will find it best to preach larger passages at a time. Likewise, when preaching through some of the books in the New Testament (e.g., Ephesians), you may find it easier to develop a sermon from a single verse at a time.

2. STUDY THE TEXT

Once you have selected a passage of scripture to preach from, the next step is to study the text. There are several tools you may use to help you study and understand a portion of scripture, including: study Bibles, commentaries, dictionaries, as well as various Bible translations.

I highly recommend that every disciple that is serious about understanding the Bible, or preaching, use a study Bible. If you do not already use one, the ESV Study Bible is a great choice. As for commentaries (e.g., Matthew Henry's Commentary, Barnes' Notes, IVP New Testament Commentary), dictionaries (e.g., Vine's Expository Dictionary of NT Words, Holman Bible Dictionary, Easton's Bible Dictionary), and other Bible translations (e.g., English Standard Version, Amplified Bible, The Message), you can find many options for free online through StudyLight.org and BibleGateway.com.

REVIEW THE PASSAGE

Once you have a passage to preach from, you can begin to study the Bible by reviewing the passage. Here is what I recommend:

1. Read the passage in multiple translations. I recommend using a word-for-word translation as your main reference. Solid

word-for-word translations include: English Standard Version (ESV), New American Standard Bible (NASB), and New King James Version (NJKV). Then you can read over paraphrased translations and easy reading translations, such as the Amplified Bible (AMP), and The Message (MSG).

2. Listen to the passage. You can use a Bible app or online resource like BibleGateway.com for this. Listening to the passage is another way to internalize it, and it is especially useful for learning how to pronounce unfamiliar words.

3. Read through the notes from a study Bible. Study Bibles have notes for many verses in the Bible, containing definitions, background information, and other insights.

4. Summarize the passage in your own words. The goal here is to formulate a concise summary statement. This is a one sentence summary of what the passage is saying. Think about it this way: if you had just 10-12 words to tell someone what the passage is about, what would you say?

DIG DEEPER FOR
GREATER UNDERSTANDING

After reading through the passage in different translations, listening to it, consulting a study Bible, and summarizing it in your own words, it is time to dig deeper to better understand the meaning of the passage. Essentially, this step is all about asking and answering a bunch of questions regarding the chosen text. Some questions to help you understand the meaning of the text are:

1. Who, or what, is this passage about?

2. What can I learn from this passage?

3. Why is this passage important?

4. How should this passage impact the way I live my daily life?

Feel free to add your own questions in there as well. There are really no limits here. The more questions you ask, the more insight you'll likely pull out. As you do this more and more, you'll begin to ask better and better questions.

You can use a Bible dictionary to look up words that need to be defined. Also, you can use a Bible concordance to find other passages that use particular words.

CHECK YOUR INTREPRETATION

After you've reviewed the text, and spent some time digging deeper for greater understanding, you'll want to review some commentaries. Commentaries are similar to what you will find in the notes of a study Bible. However, they can help you understand how others have interpreted the passage. You want to make sure you're understanding the passage correctly, and in ways that are in line with how it's historically been interpreted. This step is essentially to make sure you're not coming up with some off-the-wall interpretation.

Once you've done this, you are ready to begin considering the structure of the sermon.

3. OUTLINE THE SERMON

After studying the text, you are ready to create a sermon outline. In this stage of sermon development, you will define the goal of your sermon, formulate your main points, and write out both the introduction and the conclusion.

Before we get started, take a look at the format of an outline:

[SAMPLE SERMON OUTLINE]

Scripture:

Goal(s):

Introduction

Main Point 1

- Supporting scripture, thoughts, and stories.

Main Point 2

- Supporting scripture, thoughts, and stories.

Main Point 3

- Supporting scripture, thoughts, and stories.

Conclusion

Your completed outline is what you should have with you while you preach, as notes for reference.

DEFINE YOUR GOALS

The first thing to consider is the goal of your sermon. In light of all the insights you've discovered about your passage, what is it that you want people to walk away with after hearing your sermon? Is there something you want people to understand, to know, to recognize, to admit, to acknowledge? Are there things you want people to do in response? Are there specific changes you want them to make? You might decide on one goal or multiple goals.

Here are a few examples:

> [12] Let no one despise you for your youth, but set the believers an example in speech, in conduct, in love, in faith, in purity.
>
> 1 Timothy 4:12

Goal: I want us to be good examples.

> [1] In the spring of the year, the time when kings go out to battle, David sent Joab, and his servants with him, and all Israel. And they ravaged the Ammonites and besieged Rabbah. But David remained at Jerusalem.
>
> [2] It happened, late one afternoon, when David arose from his couch and was walking on the roof of the king's house, that he saw from the

roof a woman bathing; and the woman was very beautiful. ³ And David sent and inquired about the woman. And one said, "Is not this Bathsheba, the daughter of Eliam, the wife of Uriah the Hittite?" ⁴ So David sent messengers and took her, and she came to him, and he lay with her. (Now she had been purifying herself from her uncleanness.) Then she returned to her house. ⁵ And the woman conceived, and she sent and told David, "I am pregnant."

...

²⁶ When the wife of Uriah heard that Uriah her husband was dead, she lamented over her husband. ²⁷ And when the mourning was over, David sent and brought her to his house, and she became his wife and bore him a son. But the thing that David had done displeased the Lord.

2 Samuel 11:1-27

Goals: [1] I want us to know that anyone can fall into sin. [2] I want us to know that one sin often leads to more sin. [3] I want us to know that we cannot hide from God.

⁵⁴ Then they seized him and led him away, bringing him into the high priest's house, and Peter was following at a distance. ⁵⁵ And when they had kindled a fire in the middle of the courtyard and sat down together, Peter sat

down among them. ⁵⁶ Then a servant girl, seeing him as he sat in the light and looking closely at him, said, "This man also was with him." ⁵⁷ But he denied it, saying, "Woman, I do not know him." ⁵⁸ And a little later someone else saw him and said, "You also are one of them." But Peter said, "Man, I am not." ⁵⁹ And after an interval of about an hour still another insisted, saying, "Certainly this man also was with him, for he too is a Galilean." ⁶⁰ But Peter said, "Man, I do not know what you are talking about." And immediately, while he was still speaking, the rooster crowed. ⁶¹ And the Lord turned and looked at Peter. And Peter remembered the saying of the Lord, how he had said to him, "Before the rooster crows today, you will deny me three times." ⁶² And he went out and wept bitterly.

Luke 22:54-62

Goal: I want us to know that God can restore us.

¹⁴ "For it will be like a man going on a journey, who called his servants and entrusted to them his property. ¹⁵ To one he gave five talents, to another two, to another one, to each according to his ability. Then he went away. ¹⁶ He who had received the five talents went at once and traded with them, and he made five talents more. ¹⁷ So also he who had the two talents made two talents more. ¹⁸ But he who had

received the one talent went and dug in the ground and hid his master's money

...

26 But his master answered him, 'You wicked and slothful servant! You knew that I reap where I have not sown and gather where I scattered no seed? 27 Then you ought to have invested my money with the bankers, and at my coming I should have received what was my own with interest. 28 So take the talent from him and give it to him who has the ten talents. 29 For to everyone who has will more be given, and he will have an abundance. But from the one who has not, even what he has will be taken away. 30 And cast the worthless servant into the outer darkness. In that place there will be weeping and gnashing of teeth.'

Matthew 25:14-30

Goals: [1] I want us to know that God has entrusted us with things. [2] I want us to invest everything we have into the work of God.

While creating your goals, you want to keep your audience in mind. Remember, you are preaching to real people, with real emotions and real souls, going through very real circumstances. The more familiar you are with your audience, the more you can craft your sermon to cater to their specific needs.

You will also want to consider the spiritual maturity of your audience. Will you be preaching to a room full of church leaders? Will you be preaching to mostly non-believers or new believers? Or will you be preaching to a mixed group? You want to keep these things in mind when determining the goals for your sermon.

The audience should also determine the path you take in communicating your message. For instance, if you have mostly non-believers, you would do well to focus on relating your passage to the Gospel of Jesus Christ. Likewise, if you expect there to be a large majority of mature Christians, you might want to dig deeper into relevant theology and Christian doctrine, and couple that with practical application.

These goals you are defining for your sermon will not be voiced to the audience. These are for your reference, and they will help you create the rest of your sermon.

FORMULATE YOUR MAIN POINTS

When it comes to main points in your sermon, less if usually more. It can be argued that preaching one main point can be more effective than preaching multiple main points. If we want people to remember what we're saying, maybe the best route is to focus on just one main point and drive it home. Ultimately, this comes down to preference, and the length of time you're expected to preach. For instance, if you're preaching a typical Sunday service with a time slot of 30 minutes, a one-point message should suffice. However, if you're preaching at a conference, and your time slot is 60 minutes, you might want to add a couple more main points to make sure you have enough content.

Your main points should be determined by your sermon goals. For instance, if one of your goals is "I want us to be good examples", then one of your main points could be, "Be an example". In other words, use your main points to address the goals you have defined for the sermon.

Here are a few examples:

> 12 Let no one despise you for your youth, but set the believers an example in speech, in conduct, in love, in faith, in purity.

> 1 Timothy 4:12

Goal: I want us to be good examples.

Main Point: Be an example.

> 1 In the spring of the year, the time when kings go out to battle, David sent Joab, and his servants with him, and all Israel. And they ravaged the Ammonites and besieged Rabbah. But David remained at Jerusalem.

> 2 It happened, late one afternoon, when David arose from his couch and was walking on the roof of the king's house, that he saw from the roof a woman bathing; and the woman was

very beautiful. ³ And David sent and inquired about the woman. And one said, "Is not this Bathsheba, the daughter of Eliam, the wife of Uriah the Hittite?" ⁴ So David sent messengers and took her, and she came to him, and he lay with her. (Now she had been purifying herself from her uncleanness.) Then she returned to her house. ⁵ And the woman conceived, and she sent and told David, "I am pregnant."

...

²⁶ When the wife of Uriah heard that Uriah her husband was dead, she lamented over her husband. ²⁷ And when the mourning was over, David sent and brought her to his house, and she became his wife and bore him a son. But the thing that David had done displeased the Lord.

2 Samuel 11:1-27

Goals: [1] I want us to know that anyone can fall into sin. [2] I want us to know that one sin often leads to more sin. [3] I want us to know that we cannot hide from God.

Main Points: [1] Anyone can fall short. [2] One sin often leads to more sin. [3] We cannot hide from God.

⁵⁴ Then they seized him and led him away, bringing him into the high priest's house, and

Peter was following at a distance. ⁵⁵ And when they had kindled a fire in the middle of the courtyard and sat down together, Peter sat down among them. ⁵⁶ Then a servant girl, seeing him as he sat in the light and looking closely at him, said, "This man also was with him." ⁵⁷ But he denied it, saying, "Woman, I do not know him." ⁵⁸ And a little later someone else saw him and said, "You also are one of them." But Peter said, "Man, I am not." ⁵⁹ And after an interval of about an hour still another insisted, saying, "Certainly this man also was with him, for he too is a Galilean." ⁶⁰ But Peter said, "Man, I do not know what you are talking about." And immediately, while he was still speaking, the rooster crowed. ⁶¹ And the Lord turned and looked at Peter. And Peter remembered the saying of the Lord, how he had said to him, "Before the rooster crows today, you will deny me three times." ⁶² And he went out and wept bitterly.

Luke 22:54-62

Goal: I want us to know that God can restore us.

Main Point: It ain't over 'til it's over.

¹⁴ "For it will be like a man going on a journey, who called his servants and entrusted to them his property. ¹⁵ To one he gave five talents, to another two, to another one, to each according

to his ability. Then he went away. [16] He who had received the five talents went at once and traded with them, and he made five talents more. [17] So also he who had the two talents made two talents more. [18] But he who had received the one talent went and dug in the ground and hid his master's money

...

[26] But his master answered him, 'You wicked and slothful servant! You knew that I reap where I have not sown and gather where I scattered no seed? [27] Then you ought to have invested my money with the bankers, and at my coming I should have received what was my own with interest. [28] So take the talent from him and give it to him who has the ten talents. [29] For to everyone who has will more be given, and he will have an abundance. But from the one who has not, even what he has will be taken away. [30] And cast the worthless servant into the outer darkness. In that place there will be weeping and gnashing of teeth.'

Matthew 25:14-30

Goals: [1] I want us to know that God has entrusted us with things. [2] I want us to invest everything we have into the work of God.

Main Point: God expects a return on His investment.

When choosing your main points, remember that the main points will determine the flow of the sermon. Each main point will be a major section of your sermon, as illustrated in the sample outline. In the next chapter, you'll learn how to build out your main points, but for now, we're going to turn our attention to the other major sections of the sermon: the introduction and conclusion.

WRITE YOUR INTRODUCTION

In the introduction of your sermon, you will want to introduce the subject and scripture, and lay a foundation as to why this message is important. It is during these first few moments that the hearer makes up their mind as to whether they are going to tune in or not. This is your opportunity to grab their attention. It is often a good idea to use a story, a joke, a video, a quote, or some other illustration, as an opener.

In your introduction, you should do 3 things:

1. Address why this sermon matters. Answer the question, "Why should people listen to this message?"

2. Introduce the main scripture. Setup the passage. Share any background information or context that will help people understand the main scripture better.

3. Include a reading of the main passage of scripture. Do your best to read the passage

clearly, and smoothly. Reading the passage aloud to yourself several times before you preach should help you be prepared for this.

WRITE YOUR CONCLUSION

Perhaps the most abused part of sermons is the conclusion. Over the years, I have heard many preachers make statements like, "In conclusion... well, we all know what that means when a preacher says 'in conclusion'", implying that typical preachers have multiple conclusions, and at the same time, adding themselves to that category. This is not only a waste of time, but it detracts from the flow of the sermon. The conclusion is a pivotal point in the message. This is where the preacher wraps everything up and issues a challenge so the hearers can respond. Do not detract from this; do not disrupt the spirit, or flow, of the message with unnecessary comments like that.

The conclusion is where you'll briefly recap your main points, and then issue a challenge to the listeners. As much as you want the hearers to grow in their knowledge of the Word of God, you should also want them to mature in Christian living, and continue in the sanctification process. So therefore, always remember to challenge them to respond, inviting them to examine their lives, and if necessary, repent.

In your conclusion, you should do 3 things:

1. Briefly recap your main points. Think about what you want people to remember. Think about what you want people to be talking about after the service. If there's one thing people could walk away with, what should it be?

2. Talk about next steps. What are some next steps people should take? How should people live their lives differently, starting today? Challenge everyone to evaluate their lives based on what they just heard.

3. Share the Gospel. Find a way to incorporate the message of salvation into your conclusion. If that group of people only hears this one sermon, at least they will hear the Gospel of Jesus Christ.

You don't need to finalize your introduction and conclusion at this point. Once you write out the details of your main points, you can revisit your introduction and conclusion to make any necessary adjustments.

4. COMPLETE THE SERMON

Now that your sermon has been outlined, you can work towards completing the sermon. In this stage of sermon development, you will build out the details of your main points, and if necessary, you will revise your introduction and conclusion.

DEVELOP THE CONTENT FOR YOUR MAIN POINTS

To develop the content and details for your main points, you'll want to answer a series of questions about each main point. So, take each main point, and answer these questions:

1. How did you come to this conclusion? Walk through the passage, and show how you came up with this main point.

2. What does this mean? If your main point is, "Be an example", ask yourself, "What does it mean to be an example?"

3. Why is this important? Explain why this should matter to people.

4. What are some struggles, or obstacles, or objections, people may have regarding this? Acknowledge these and offer a response.

5. How do we live this out? Think about what this looks like practically. Consider how this should impact the way we live our daily lives.

As you're answering these questions, feel free to use other scriptures and personal stories to help you explain and illustrate your answers.

If you refer back to the sample sermon outline in the previous chapter, you can use the answers to the above questions as bullet points under the main points. In the sample sermon outline, this part is labeled as "Supporting scripture, thoughts, and stories."

FINALIZE YOUR INTRODUCTION AND CONCLUSION

After the content for your main points has been written, review your introduction and conclusion. Does it flow well? Does it all fit together? If you feel you need to make some adjustments, then go right ahead. Sometimes, developing the content for our main points brings forth new, or different, ideas for the introduction and conclusion.

SECTION 1:
IN A NUTSHELL

1. Select a passage of scripture.

2. Use various Bible translations and Bible study tools to study the text.

3. Considering your audience, define any goals for this sermon.

4. In light of the goals for the sermon, formulate your main points.

5. Create a sermon outline, mapping out the major parts of the sermon, including: the introduction, the main points, and the conclusion.

6. Write and finalize the content for each section of the sermon.

Throughout this whole process, be in prayer. Pray for the people you will be ministering to, pray for an anointing, and pray about the message. More important than anything else is that you hear from God, and you communicate all that He wants you to say.

SECTION 2:
SERMON DELIVERY

5. PREPARATION

In general, when speaking in public, one of the most important things you can do is be as prepared as possible. This means knowing the material. If you are good at memorization, I would recommend trying to memorize at least your opening line, your main points, and your closing line. Then, of course, you can use your sermon outline for reference during your delivery.

Here are some keys to being prepared to preach:

1. Read the scripture(s) over and over again.

2. Memorize your opening line, your main points, and your closing line.

3. Pray for wisdom, anointing, and power from God.

6. TIME MANAGEMENT

When it comes to time management, there are two things to be aware of: [1] the time slot you have been given, and [2] time sensitivity.

TIME SLOT

When you are invited to preach, you will likely be given a time slot. If you are not directly given a time slot, there is usually an implied time slot. Churches vary on their average sermon length. Some churches prefer an hour-long sermon every service, while others stick to a thirty-minute message. It is the job of the preacher to understand the appropriate time slot, and deliver in the designated time frame.

Managing your pulpit time is a skill that develops with experience. This skill can become quite challenging to improve on, depending on your personality. For those who are talkative, and drag things out in everyday conversation, you might need to learn to condense your sermon material. Likewise, for those who are more reserved, and short with their words, you might need to learn to expand your message to fit the appropriate time slot.

It is important to always be considerate of the time slot you have been given. Try to go the full length, but don't go over. Be respectful of the hearers and their time. There is no reason other people should have to monitor your time. No one should have to worry about how much longer you'll go over if they don't cut you off. Be respectful, or you'll likely lose out on many opportunities to minister.

TIME SENSITIVITY

Every second of every minute counts. Therefore, make the best use of the time you've been given. Do not waste time with unnecessary thanksgiving to the pastor for allowing you to minister. Do not waste time saying "Amen" after every 3 words, or saying, "Oh, when I heard I was going to preach today, I started praying and asking God what He wanted me to say...". Get to the point; get right to it. As a side note, saying "Amen" or "Hallelujah" after every other word is unintelligible. Consider how you sound to those listening in the congregation, and to those who may listen to your recording online. Speak intelligibly, and you'll likely see more doors open for you.

Lastly, be mindful of the important parts of your stories, and your illustrations in general. If I am telling a story about my wife being told she was going to die in the hospital while giving birth to our son, I don't need to include unnecessary details. There is no need for me to explain how she got pregnant, or when she got pregnant, or what we ate for breakfast. In other words, get to the point.

7. COMPOSURE

Maintain composure, even if you feel nervous, or lose your place, or lose focus, or can't find the right words. Maintain composure. Avoid saying things like, "Uh, uh, uh, I can't find my place", "Uhhhh, where was I?" For example, if you lose your place, simply find your spot in your sermon outline, and continue when you are ready. Furthermore, you must learn to control yourself when the audience communicates back. When you are in front of a group preaching, sometimes you will see people yawning, laughing, talking, walking out, and so forth. In such cases, it is important to maintain composure. Stay in control of your message.

8. BODY LANGUAGE

Be mindful of your body language. The way that you present yourself, and the movements you make (or don't make), have a tremendous impact on the overall effectiveness of your delivery. Here are some things to consider:

- Make eye contact with as many people as you can throughout the message.

- Learn to stop and breathe. Pauses in speech and in movement can add dramatic emphasis.

- Make appropriate gestures. When you are talking about something going down, you don't want to raise your hands up high in the air. Incorporate hand gestures for sure, but use them appropriately.

- Try to avoid nervous tics, like fiddling with the microphone cable.

9. AUTHORITY

When you are behind the pulpit, you are looked at as a leader, as someone who has knowledge, someone who has wisdom, someone who has experience, and someone that people should listen to, someone to learn from. So act accordingly. When you are preaching, remember, you are the man (or woman) of God for that time. Act and walk in that authority.

Don't lose credibility. Don't say things like, "Sorry, I'm not as good as Pastor", or "I can't teach like Bob". Don't say those things. Don't put yourself down, or talk like you don't know what you're saying. When you make statements like that, it makes people wonder why they should listen to what you have to say.

What will help you to preach with authority is having confidence in your understanding of the scripture(s) you are preaching. Therefore, I would recommend that you do your due diligence in studying, and understanding what the scripture says, and gleaning from other people's interpretation of it.

10. HUMILITY

Sometimes, as a preacher, you will find that others look at you in high regard. Your hearers will sometimes assume that you have it all together, that you are doing everything right, reading and praying all the time, living a blessed and holy life. And in some regards, that should be true of you. However, the danger is that when you preach, you can begin to talk at people, rather than including yourself with them. As such, you might tend to refrain from exposing any faults or sin that you have dealt with. Listen, do not be afraid to expose faults in your life, or things that you have struggled with, or even sin. People like to follow real people. It is comforting and reassuring to know that your leaders have gone through similar situations, and have dealt with similar sins. You are not above anyone. You may be at a different level in the sanctification process, but nevertheless, you are in need of Jesus and the Holy Spirit just as much as anyone else.

With that said, avoid using words like, "you", or "you guys", or "you people". Instead, include yourself by saying, "we" and "us". For example, you don't want to say, "You guys need to change." Rather, it would be better to say, "We need to change." Doing so puts everyone on the same level, and demonstrates your acknowledgement that everyone can use some improvement.

Be humble, and watch out for prideful thoughts and motives that might creep in.

SECTION 2:
IN A NUTSHELL

1. Be as prepared as possible.

2. Know the time slot you have been given.

3. Don't waste time while you are preaching.

4. Maintain composure.

5. Use appropriate body language.

6. Preach with authority.

7. Speak in humility.

NEXT STEPS

There are so many great resources available that can take you to the next level, and help you become an even better preacher. When you are ready to take some next steps, I have a few books I'd like to recommend:

1. *Living By The Book* by Howard G. Hendricks & William D. Hendricks

2. *Communicating For A Change* by Andy Stanley & Ronald Lane Jones

3. *Power In The Pulpit: How To Prepare And Deliver Expository Sermons* by Jerry Vines & Jim Shaddix

ABOUT THE AUTHOR

Chad Meza is a pastor, church planter, songwriter, and author serving at Activate Church in California. His heart is to make disciples and proclaim the truth of God's Word with clarity.

If you have any questions or comments, feel free to contact Chad Meza at hello@chadmeza.com.

Made in the USA
Middletown, DE
23 September 2023

39146598R00038